هَلْ دَعَوْتَ لِأَوْلَادِكَ؟

Have You Prayed for Your Children?

A Prayer Book for Every Parent

Abu Ameenah Ma'ruf Orewole, PhD

Have You Prayed Children? A Prayer Book for Every Parent.

ISBN

ISBN: 9798827742876

+2348056683255

morewole@gmail.com

Contents

Introduction

Alhamdulillah for all His favours among which is the gift of children.

الْمَالُ وَالْبَنُونَ زِينَةُ الْحَيَاةِ الدُّنْيَا

"Wealth and children are the adornment of this worldly life" **(Qur'ān 18: 46)**

They are also a source of fitnah.

وَاعْلَمُوا أَنَّمَا أَمْوَالُكُمْ وَأَوْلَادُكُمْ فِتْنَةٌ

"And know that your properties and your children are but a trial." **(Qur'ān 8:28)**

May Allāh's blessings be upon Prophet Muhammad (ﷺ), his household and his companions and all followers of the truth till the day of Judgment.

The children are the comfort of the parents' eyes, and a source of delight. Why will you not pray to have them or pray for the best for them if you are already blessed by Allāh?!

It is however observed that some parents out of sheer ignorance or negligence, instead of praying for their children are cursing them when they do something that annoys them. This is against the Sunnah of the Prophet (ﷺ) as he was reported to have said on the authority of Jabir (ؓ):

"لا تدعوا على أنفسكم، ولا تدعوا على أولادكم، ولا تدعو على أموالكم، لا توافقوا من الله ساعة يسأل فيها عطاء، فيستجيب لكم".

"Do not invoke curses on yourself or on your children or on your possessions lest you should happen to do it at a moment when the supplications are accepted, and your prayer might be granted." [Muslim].

However, it is part of Allah's mercy that the supplication of parents against their children at the time of anger and boredom are not answered. Allāh says[1]:

وَلَوْ يُعَجِّلُ اللَّهُ لِلنَّاسِ الشَّرَّ اسْتِعْجَالَهُم بِالْخَيْرِ لَقُضِيَ إِلَيْهِمْ أَجَلُهُمْ ۖ فَنَذَرُ الَّذِينَ لَا يَرْجُونَ لِقَاءَنَا فِي طُغْيَانِهِمْ يَعْمَهُونَ

***"And if Allah was to hasten for the people the evil [they invoke] as He hastens for them the good, their term would have been ended for them. But We leave the ones who do not expect the meeting with Us, in their transgression, wandering blindly"* (Qur'ān 10: 11)**

What is expected from parents is to supplicate for their children to be guided and for Allāh to reform them and inspire them to guidance. The Prophet (ﷺ) said:

---

[1]Shaykh Ibn Katheer, may God have mercy on him, in his Tafsir (2/554) of this verse: Almighty Allāh mentions His forbearance and kindness to His servants, and that He does not respond to them if they supplicate against themselves, their money, or their children, when they are bored and angry because He knows that they are not determined on that evil, so He does not respond to them in this situation. This is out of His kindness and mercy. However, He responds to them if they supplicate for themselves, their money, or their children, with goodness, blessing and progress.

"ثَلاَثُ دَعَوَاتٍ يُسْتَجَابُ لَهُنَّ لاَ شَكَّ فِيهِنَّ دَعْوَةُ الْمَظْلُومِ وَدَعْوَةُ الْمُسَافِرِ وَدَعْوَةُ الْوَالِدِ لِوَلَدِهِ".

"There are three supplications that will undoubtedly be answered: the supplication of one who has been wronged; the supplication of the traveler; and the supplication of a father for his child."[2] [Ibn Majah]

Have you prayed for your children? is a collection of prayers for every parent to supplicate to Allāh for their children for the good of this world and the hereafter. You may select appropriately or read the whole collection.

May Allāh grant us righteous progeny and answer our supplications for our children.

Abu Ameenah Ma`ruf Orewole, PhD
Jumadal Ūla, 1443 A.H. (December 2021)

---

[2] Ibn Majah 3862, and classed as *hasan* by al-Albaani in *Silsilat,* 596.

Evidences on Praying for Progeny

There are evidences from the Qur'ān and Sunnah on supplicating to Allāh for righteous progeny. Some of them will be cited here:

1. Prophet Ibrahim and Ismail (ﷺ) called on their Lord and prayed for their progeny to remain Muslims. Prophet (ﷺ) Muhammad was reported to have said that: *"I am the response to the supplication of my father."*[3]

وَإِذْ يَرْفَعُ إِبْرَاهِيمُ الْقَوَاعِدَ مِنَ الْبَيْتِ وَإِسْمَاعِيلُ رَبَّنَا تَقَبَّلْ مِنَّا ۖ إِنَّكَ أَنتَ السَّمِيعُ الْعَلِيمُ ﴿١٢٧﴾ رَبَّنَا وَاجْعَلْنَا مُسْلِمَيْنِ لَكَ وَمِن ذُرِّيَّتِنَا أُمَّةً مُّسْلِمَةً لَّكَ وَأَرِنَا مَنَاسِكَنَا وَتُبْ عَلَيْنَا ۖ إِنَّكَ أَنتَ التَّوَّابُ الرَّحِيمُ ﴿١٢٨﴾ رَبَّنَا وَابْعَثْ فِيهِمْ رَسُولًا مِّنْهُمْ يَتْلُو عَلَيْهِمْ آيَاتِكَ وَيُعَلِّمُهُمُ الْكِتَابَ وَالْحِكْمَةَ وَيُزَكِّيهِمْ ۚ إِنَّكَ أَنتَ الْعَزِيزُ الْحَكِيمُ ﴿١٢٩﴾

And [mention] when Abraham was raising the foundations of the House and [with him] Ishmael, [saying], "Our Lord, accept [this] from us. Indeed You are the Hearing, the Knowing. Our Lord, and make us Muslims [in submission] to You and from our descendants a Muslim nation [in submission] to You. And show us our rites and accept our repentance. Indeed, You are the Accepting of repentance,

---

[3] Ibn Hisham, Sira: 1/175; Tabari, Tarikh: 2/128.

the Merciful. Our Lord, and send among them a messenger from themselves who will recite to them Your verses and teach them the Book and wisdom and purify them. Indeed, You are the Exalted in Might, the Wise." (Qur'ān 2: 127-129)

2. Prophet Lūt (ﷺ) prayed for the salvation and safety of his household.

قَالُوا لَئِن لَّمْ تَنتَهِ يَا لُوطُ لَتَكُونَنَّ مِنَ الْمُخْرَجِينَ ﴿١٦٧﴾ قَالَ إِنِّي لِعَمَلِكُم مِّنَ الْقَالِينَ ﴿١٦٨﴾ رَبِّ نَجِّنِي وَأَهْلِي مِمَّا يَعْمَلُونَ ﴿١٦٩﴾ فَنَجَّيْنَاهُ وَأَهْلَهُ أَجْمَعِينَ ﴿١٧٠﴾

They said, "If you do not desist, O Lot, you will surely be of those evicted." He said, "Indeed, I am, toward your deed, of those who detest [it]. My Lord, save me and my family from [the consequence of] what they do." So We saved him and his family, all. (Qur'ān 26: 167-170)

3. The Mother of wife of Imran and mother of Maryam (ﷺ) prayed dedicated her unborn child to Allāh and prayed for her progeny.

إِذْ قَالَتِ امْرَأَتُ عِمْرَانَ رَبِّ إِنِّي نَذَرْتُ لَكَ مَا فِي بَطْنِي مُحَرَّرًا فَتَقَبَّلْ مِنِّي ۖ إِنَّكَ أَنتَ السَّمِيعُ الْعَلِيمُ ﴿٣٥﴾ فَلَمَّا وَضَعَتْهَا قَالَتْ رَبِّ إِنِّي وَضَعْتُهَا أُنثَىٰ وَاللَّهُ أَعْلَمُ بِمَا وَضَعَتْ وَلَيْسَ الذَّكَرُ كَالْأُنثَىٰ ۖ وَإِنِّي سَمَّيْتُهَا مَرْيَمَ وَإِنِّي أُعِيذُهَا بِكَ وَذُرِّيَّتَهَا مِنَ الشَّيْطَانِ الرَّجِيمِ ﴿٣٦﴾

[Mention, O Muhammad], when the wife of 'Imran said, "My Lord, indeed I have pledged to You what is in my womb, consecrated [for Your service], so accept this from me. Indeed, You are the Hearing, the Knowing." But when she delivered her, she said, "My Lord, I have delivered a female." And Allah was most knowing of what she delivered, "And the male is not like the female. And I have named her Mary, and I seek refuge for her in You and [for] her descendants from Satan, the expelled [from the mercy of Allah]." (Qur'ān 3: 35-36)

4. Prophet Zakariyyah (ﷺ) prayed for righteous progeny.

هُنَالِكَ دَعَا زَكَرِيَّا رَبَّهُ ۖ قَالَ رَبِّ هَبْ لِي مِن لَّدُنكَ ذُرِّيَّةً طَيِّبَةً ۖ إِنَّكَ سَمِيعُ الدُّعَاءِ ﴿٣٨﴾ فَنَادَتْهُ الْمَلَائِكَةُ وَهُوَ قَائِمٌ يُصَلِّي فِي الْمِحْرَابِ أَنَّ اللَّهَ يُبَشِّرُكَ بِيَحْيَىٰ مُصَدِّقًا بِكَلِمَةٍ مِّنَ اللَّهِ وَسَيِّدًا وَحَصُورًا وَنَبِيًّا مِّنَ الصَّالِحِينَ ﴿٣٩﴾

At that, Zechariah called upon his Lord, saying, "My Lord, grant me from Yourself a good offspring. Indeed, You are the Hearer of supplication." So the angels called him while he was standing in prayer in the chamber, "Indeed, Allah gives you good tidings of John, confirming a word from Allah and [who will be] honorable, abstaining [from women], and a prophet from among the righteous." (Qur'ān 3: 38-39)

5. Prophet Muhammad (ﷺ) was blessed with a special prayer meant for himself, his household and progeny till the day of judgment. It is called the Solaatu Ibrahimiyah.

(اللَّهُمَّ صَلِّ عَلَى مُحَمَّدٍ وَعَلَى أَزْوَاجِهِ وَذُرِّيَّتِهِ، كَمَا صَلَّيْتَ عَلَى آلِ إِبْرَهِيمِ، وَبَارِكْ عَلَى مُحَمَّدٍ وَعَلَى أَزْوَاجِهِ وَذُرِّيَّتِهِ، كَمَا بَارَكْتَ عَلَى آلِ إِبْرَهِيمِ، إِنَّكَ حَمِيدٌ مَجِيدٌ)

O Allāh, send prayers upon Muhammad and upon the wives and descendants of Muhammad, just as You sent prayers upon the family of Ibrahiim, and send blessings upon Muhammad and upon the wives and descendants of Muhammad, just as You sent blessings upon the family of Ibrahiim. Verily, You are full of praise and majesty.[4]

عَنْ أَبِي هُرَيْرَةَ، أَنَّ رَسُولَ اللَّهِ صلى الله عليه وسلم قَالَ " لِكُلِّ نَبِيٍّ دَعْوَةٌ يَدْعُو بِهَا فَأُرِيدُ أَنْ أَخْتَبِئَ دَعْوَتِي شَفَاعَةً لأُمَّتِي فِي الآخِرَةِ " .

Abu Hurayra narrated that the Messenger of Allāh (ﷺ) said, "Every prophet is given a supplication (dua), and I wish to preserve my dua as intercession for my community in the next world." [Muwatta, Book 15, Hadith 498]

"إذا مات الأنسان انقطع عمله إلا من ثلاث: صدقة جارية، أو علم ينتفع به، أو ولد صالح يدعو له" (رواه مسلم).

Abu Hurairah (ؓ) reported: The Messenger of Allah (ﷺ) said, *"When a man dies, his deeds come to an end, except for three: A continuous charity, knowledge by which people derive benefit, pious son who prays for him."* [Muslim].

The prayer of a believing parent is not for only his or her biological children alone. You need to pray for your step-children, your maids and everyone under your care. An

---

[4] *Allahumma salli 'ala Muhammadin wa 'ala azwaajihi wa dhurriyatihi, kamaa sallaita 'ala aali Ibrahiima. Wa baarik 'ala Muhammadin wa 'ala azwaajihi wa dhurriyatihi, kamaa baarakta 'ala aali Ibrahiima, innaka Hamiidun Majiid.*

excellent example is the case of Umm Sulaim, the mother of Anas, whom she dedicated to the service of the Prophet (ﷺ). She requested that the Prophet (ﷺ) pray for Anas, her son.

Anas (ﷺ) reported that Umm Sulaim said: O Allah's Messenger, here is your servant Anas, invoke blessings of Allah upon him. Thereupon he (the Holy Prophet ﷺ) said:

﴿اللَّهُمَّ أَكْثِرْ مَالَهُ وَوَلَدَهُ وَبَارِكْ لَهُ فِيمَا أَعْطَيْتَهُ﴾

Allahumma akthir maalahu wa waladahu wa baarik lahu fiimaa a`ataitahu.

O Allah, make an increase in his wealth, and progeny, and confer blessings upon him in everything Thou hast bestowed upon him. [Bukhārī and Muslim]

This page is intentionally left blank

دُعَاءٌ لِلأَوْلَادِ

Prayers for the Children

1. Prayer for guidance and obedience

﴿رَبَّنَا هَبْ لَنَا مِنْ أَزْوَاجِنَا وَذُرِّيَّاتِنَا قُرَّةَ أَعْيُنٍ وَاجْعَلْنَا لِلْمُتَّقِينَ إِمَامًا﴾

1. Rabbanaa hab lanaa min 'azwaajinaa wadh-dhurriyaatinaa qurrata a'ayunin, waj'alnaa lil muttaqiina imaaman.

Our Lord ! bestow on us from our wives and our offspring the comfort of our eyes, and make us leaders of the pious (Qur'ān 25: 74).

﴿رَبِّ اجْعَلْنِي مُقِيمَ الصَّلَاةِ وَمِنْ ذُرِّيَّتِي رَبَّنَا وَتَقَبَّلْ دُعَاءِ * رَبَّنَا اغْفِرْ لِي وَلِوَالِدَيَّ وَلِلْمُؤْمِنِينَ يَوْمَ يَقُومُ الْحِسَابُ﴾

2. Rabbi-j'alnii muqiimas-solaati wa min dhuriyyatii Rabbanaa wa taqobbal duaa'i. Rabbanagfir lii waliwaalidayya walil-mu'miniina yaoma yaquumul hisaabu. (Qur'ān 14: 40)

My Lord, make me an establisher of prayer, and [many] from my descendants. Our Lord, and accept my supplication. Our Lord, forgive me and my parents and the believers the Day the account is established.

﴿اللَّهُمَّ وَفِّقْ أَوْلَادِي لِمَا تُحِبُّهُ وَتَرْضَاهُ، اللَّهُمَّ ارْزُقْهُمْ حِفْظَ النَّبِيِّينَ، وَفَهْمَ الْمُرْسَلِينَ﴾

3. Allahuma waffiq aolaadii limaa tuhibbuhu watardoohu, Allahumma rzuqu-hum hifzan-nabbiyyiina, wa fahmal mursaliina.

O Allāh! Guide my children to what You love and are pleased with. O Allāh! Grant them the protection of the Prophets, and the understanding of the Messengers.

﴿اللَّهُمَّ احْفَظْ لِي أَوْلَادِي وَوَفِّقْهُمْ لِطَاعَتِكَ، وَبَارِكْ لِي فِيهِمْ﴾

4. Allahumma-hfaz lii aolaadii wawafiq-hum li too'atika, wabaarik lii fiihim.

O Allāh! Protect my children for me, guide them to your obedience and bless me with them.

﴿اللَّهُمَّ حَبِّبْ إِلَيْهِمُ الإِيمَانَ وَزَيِّنْهُ فِي قُلُوبِهِمْ، وَكَرِّهْ إِلَيْهِمُ الْكُفْرَ وَالْفُسُوقَ وَالْعِصْيَانَ، وَاجْعَلْهُمْ مِنَ الرَّاشِدِينَ﴾

5. Allahumma habbib ilaihimul iimaana wa zayyinhu fii quluubihim, wakarrih ilaihimul kufra wal fusuuqa wal `isyaana, waj'al-hum minar-raashidiina.

O Allāh! Kindly endear the faith to them and beautify it in their hearts. Make disbelief and lewdness and rebellion hateful unto them and make them of the rightly guided.

﴿اللَّهُمَّ إِنِّي أَسْأَلُكَ بِأَسْمَائِكَ الْحُسْنَى وَصِفَاتِكَ الْعُلْيَا أَنْ تَجْعَلَ أَوْلَادِي هُدَاةً مُهْتَدِينَ﴾

6. Allahumma innii as'aluka bi asmaa'ikal husnaa wa sifaatikal `ulyaa an taj`al aolaadii hudaatan muhtadiin.

O Allāh! I beseech You with Your Beautiful Names and Noble Attributes to make my children a guide for the guided ones.

2. Prayer for honourable status before Allāh

﴿اللَّهُمَّ إِنِّي أَسْأَلُكَ أَنْ تَجْعَلَ أَبْنَائِي مِنَ النَّاجِحِينَ الْمُتَفَوِقِينَ، اللَّهُمَّ وَفِّقْهُمْ وَكُنْ مَعَهُمْ، اللَّهُمَّ ارْزُقْهُمْ أَعْلَى الدَّرَجَاتِ، وَأَرْفَعِ الْمَنَاصِبَ﴾

7. Allahuma innii as'aluka an taj`al abnaa'ii minal naaji-hiinal mutafawiqiina. Allahuma wafiqhum wa kun ma`a-hum. Allahuma rzuqu-hum a'alaad- darajaati, wa 'arfa`al manaasiba.

O Allāh! I ask you to make my children among the successful and outstanding. O Allāh! Guide them and be with them. O Allāh! Grant them the highest degrees, and the highest positions.

﴿اللَّهُمَّ اجْعَلْهُمْ أَوْفَرَ عِبَادِكَ حَظًّا فِي الدُّنْيَا وَالآخِرَةِ، وَاجْعَلْهُمْ مِنْ أَوْلِيَائِكَ وَخَاصَّتِكَ، الَّذِينَ يَسْعَى نُورُهُمْ بَيْنَ أَيْدِيهِمْ وَبِأَيْمَانِهِمْ﴾

8. Allahumma j'al-hum aofara `ibadika hazzan fii duniya wal aakhirati, waj'al-hum min aoliyaaika wa khassatika lladhiina yas'aa nuuruhum baina aidii-him wa bi aimaani-him.

O Allāh! Make them the most fortunate among your servants in this world and in the Hereafter, and make them among your allies and special friends, whose lights are shining in their fronts and in their right sides.

﴿اللَّهُمَّ فَرِّحْ بِهِمْ نَبِيَّكَ الْمُخْتَارَ، وَأَعْلِ بِهِمُ الْمَنَارَ، يَا عَزِيزُ يَا غَفَّارُ﴾

9. Allahumma farih bihim nabiyyakal mukhtaar, wa a'al bihimul manaara, Yaa `Aziizu Yaa Ghaffaar.

O Allah, grant them delight in Your chosen Prophet, and raise the light with them, O Mighty, O Forgiving.

﴿اللَّهُمَّ اجْعَلْهُمْ مِمَّنْ تَوَاضَعَ لَكَ فَرَفَعْتَهُ، وَاسْتَكَانَ لِهَيْبَتِكَ فَأَحْبَبْتَهُ، وَتَقَرَّبَ إِلَيْكَ فَقَرَّبْتَهُ وَسَأَلَكَ فَأَجَبْتَهُ﴾

10.   Allahumma j'al-hum miman tawaado'a laka fa raf'ata-hum, wastakaana li'haibatika fa hababtahu, wa taqarraba ilaika faqarrabtahu, wa sa' alaka fa ajabtahu.

O Allāh! Make them among those who humbled before You and You raised him up, and subdued himself to Your Majesty, so You loved him, and he drew near to you, and You drew him close, and he supplicated to You and You answered.

﴿اللَّهُمَّ آتِ نُفُوسَهُمْ تَقْوَاهَا، وَزَكِّهَا أَنْتَ خَيْرُ مَنْ زَكَّاهَا، وَاجْعَلْهُمْ أَبْرَارًا أَتْقِيَاءَ، بُصَرَاءَ سَامِعِينَ وَلَكَ مُطِيعِينَ، وَلِأَوْلِيَائِكَ مُحِبِّينَ وَلِأَعْدَائِكَ مُبْغِضِينَ﴾

11.   Allahumma aati nufusa-hum taqwahaa, wa zakkihaa, anta khairu man zakkahaa, waj'al-hum abraran atqiyaa'a, busoroo'a saami`iina wa laka muti`iina, wal-aoliyaaika muhibbina wal a'adaaika mubghidiina.

O Allāh! Grant them piety, and increase it, for You are the best to increase it, and make them righteous, pious, obedient, attentive and obedient to You, and loving Your friends and hating Your enemies.

3. Prayer for knowledge, wisdom and retentive memory

اللَّهُمَّ يَا مُعَلِّمَ مُوسَى –عَلَيْهِ السَّلاَم– عَلِّمْهُمْ، وَيَا مُفَهِّمَ سُلَيْمَانَ – عَلَيْهِ السَّلاَم – فَهِّمْهُمْ، وَيَا مُؤْتِيَ لُقْمَانَ وَدَاوُدَ الْحِكْمَةَ وَفَصْلَ الْخِطَابِ، آتِيهِمُ الْحِكْمَةَ وَفَصْلَ الْخِطَاب

12. *Allahumma Yaa Mu`allima Muusaa – alaihis-salaam - `alllim-hum; Wa Yaa Mufahhima Sulaimaana – alaihis-salaam - fahhim-hum; Wa Yaa Mu'tiya Luqmaan wa Daawuda-l-hikmata wa fasla-l-khitoobi, aatihimu-l-hikmata wa fasla-l-khitoobi.*

O Allāh! The Teacher of Musa - peace be upon him - teach them, and O The Giver of understanding to Sulaiman - peace be upon him – give them understanding, and O The Bestower of wisdom and clear speech to Luqman and Dawud, bestow them with wisdom and clear speech.

اللَّهُمَّ عَلِّمْهُمْ مَا جَهِلُوا، وَذَكِّرْهُمْ مَا نَسُوا، وَافْتَحْ عَلَيْهِمْ مِنْ بَرَكَاتِ السَّمَاءِ وَالأَرْضِ إِنَّكَ سَمِيعُ الدُّعَاءِ

13. *Allahummu `ullim-hum maa juhiluu, wa dhakkir-hum maa nasuu, waftah `alaihim barakaati-s-samaai wal-ardi innaka Samii`u-d-duaa.*

O Allāh! Teach them what they do not know, remind them what they forget and open the blessings of the heavens and the earth for them. You are the Hearer of supplications.

﴿اللَّهُمَّ إِنِّي أَسْأَلُكَ لَهُمْ قُوَّةَ الْحِفْظِ، وَسُرْعَةَ الْفَهْمِ، وَصَفَاءَ الذِّهْنِ، اللَّهُمَّ اجْعَلْهُمْ هُدَاةً مُهْتَدِينَ﴾

14.   *Allahumma innii as'aluka lahum quwatal hifz, wa sur`atal fahmi, wa sofaa'a-d-dhihni, Allahumma-j'alhum hudaatan muhtadiin.*

O Allāh! I beseech You for power of retentive memory for them, quick understanding, sharp intelligence. O Allāh make them the guide for the guided ones.

﴿اللَّهُمَّ اجْعَلْهُمْ حَفَظَةً لِكَتَابِكَ، وَدُعَاةً وَمُجَاهِدِينَ فِي سَبِيلِكَ، وَمُبَلِّغِينَ عَنْ رَسُولِكَ مُحَمَّدٍ ﷺ﴾

15.   *Allhumma ij'alhum hafadhatan li kitābika wa du'ātan wa mujaahidiina fii sabiilika wa muballigiina 'an Rasuulika Muhammad (ﷺ).*

O Allah! Make them of those who memorize your book, callers to Your path and strivers on it, and bearer of the message from Your Messenger (ﷺ).

﴿اللَّهُمَّ افْتَحْ عَلَيْهِمْ فُتُوحَ الْعَارِفِينَ، وَارْزُقْهُمُ الْحِكْمَةَ وَالْعِلْمَ النَّافِعَ، وَزَيِّنْ أَخْلَاقَهُمْ بِالْحِلْمِ، وَأَكْرِمْهُمْ بِالتَّقْوَى، وَجَمِّلْهُمْ بِالْعَافِيَةِ﴾

16.   *Allahumma ftah alaihim futuuhal 'aarifiin, warzuku-humul hikmata wal 'ilman-naafi'a wa zayyin akhlaaqo-hum bil hilmi, wa akrim-hum bit-taqwaa wa jammil-hum bil 'aafiyah.*

O Allah! Open to them the access to the knowledge of the learned and grant them wisdom and beneficial knowledge, beautify their character with tolerance, honour them with piety, and adorn them with sound health.

﴾اللَّهُمَّ اجْعَلِ الْقُرْآنَ الْعَظِيمَ رَبِيعَ قُلُوبِهِمْ، وَشِفَاءَ صُدُورِهِمْ، وَنُورَ أَبْصَارِهِمْ، وَذَهَابَ أَحْزَانِهِمْ﴾

17.   *Allahumma j'alil-Qurānal 'adhiima rabii'a quluubihim, wa shifaa-a suduuri him, wa nuuran absoori-him, wa dhahaaba ahzaanihim.*

O Allāh! Make the Glorious Qur'ān the spring of their hearts, the healing for all (ailments) in their bosoms, and light in their vision, and the departure of their sorrow.

4. Prayer for healing from all diseases

﴾اللَّهُمَّ اشفِ أَوْلَادِي شِفَاءً تَامًّا لَا يُغَادِرُهُ سَقَمًا، اللَّهُمَّ أَسْبِغْ عَلَيْهِمْ عَافِيَةً مِنْ عِنْدِكَ، وَأَبْعِدْ عَنْهُمْ كُلَّ مَا يُؤْذِيهِمْ يَا رَبَّ الْعَالَمِينَ﴾

18.   *Allahuma shfi aolaadi shifaa'an taaman laa yughadiruhu saqman, Allahuma 'asbagh `alaihim `aafiyatan min `indika, wa `ab`id `an-hum kulla maa yu'dhii-him Yaa Rabbal `Aalamina.*

O Allāh! Heal my children completely without leaving behind any sickness. O Allāh! Grant them wellness from You, and keep them away from everything that harms them, O Lord of the worlds.

﴾اللَّهُمَّ امْنِنْ عَلَى أَوْلَادِي بِالشِّفَاءِ، وَاحْفَظْهُمْ مِنْ كُلِّ مَكْرُوهٍ، وَأَبْعِدْ عَنْهُمْ كُلَّ دَاءٍ وَسَقَمٍ، إِنَّكَ الْقَادِرُ عَلَى ذَلِكَ وَوَلِيُّهُ﴾

19.   *Allahuma amnin `alaa aolaadii bish-shifaa'i, wahfaz-hum min kulla makruuhi, wa ab`id `an-hum kulla daa'in wa saqamin, innakal qaadir `alaa dhaalika wa waliyyuhu.*

O Allāh! Grant healing to my children, protect them from every misfortune, and keep them away from every disease and sickness, for You are the One who is able to do that and his Guardian.

﴿اللَّهُمَّ اكْفِهِمْ شَرَّ الأَوْرَامِ وَالأَسْقَامِ، اللَّهُمَّ مَتِّعْهِمْ بِالصِّحَّةِ وَالْعَافِيَةِ، وَالْمَعَافَاةِ الدَّائِمَةِ فِي الدِّينِ وَالدُّنْيَا وَالآخِرَةِ﴾

20. Allahumma kfihim sharrol aoraam wal asqoomi, Allahumma matti`i-him bis-sihhati wal `aafiyati, wal mu`aafaatid-daa'imati fid-diini wad-duniyaa wal-aakhirati.

Oh God, protect them from the evil of tumors and diseases, God bless them with health, wellness, sound and enduring wellbeing in the religion, worldly affairs and hereafter.

5. Prayer for success in this life and hereafter

﴿اللَّهُمَّ اجْعَلْ أَوْلَادِي مِنْ أَسْعَدِ خَلْقِكَ، اللَّهُمَّ ارْزُقْهُمْ سَعَادَةَ الدُّنْيَا، وَارْزُقْهُمْ سَعَادَةَ الآخِرَةِ، وَافْتَحْ لَهُمْ أَبْوَابَ رَحْمَتِكَ وَفَضْلِكَ يَا ذَا الْجَلَالِ وَالإِكْرَامِ﴾

21. Allahuma j'al aolaadi min as`adi khalqika. Allahuma rzuqu-hum sa`aadatad-duniya, warzuqu-hum sa'aadatal aakhirati, waftah lahum abwaaba rahmatika wa fadlika Yaa dhal jalaali wal ikraam.

O Allāh! Make my children among the happiest of Your creation. O Allāh! Grant them the happiness of this world, and grant them the happiness of the Hereafter, and open for them the doors of Your mercy and grace, O Lord of Majesty and Honour.

﴿اللّٰهُمَّ اجْعَلْهُمْ مِنَ الْمُوَسَّعِ عَلَيْهِمْ فِي الرِّزْقِ الْحَلَالِ، الْمُعَوَّذِينَ مِنَ الذُّلِّ إِلاَّ لَكَ، وَالْمُجَارِينَ مِنَ الظُّلْمِ بِعَدْلِكَ، وَالْمُعَافِينَ مِنَ الْبَلَاءِ بِرَحْمَتِكَ﴾

22.   Allahumma j'alhum minal muwassa`i `alaihim fir-rizqil halaali, al-mu`awwadhiina minadh-dhulli illa laka, wal-mujaariina minaz-zulmi bi `adlika, wal-mu`aafiina minal-balaa'i bi rahmatika.

O Allah, make them among those who are enlarged with regard to lawful sustenance, those who seek refuge from humiliation except for you. And those who are preserved from oppression by Your justice, and those who are saved from affliction by Your mercy.

﴿اللّٰهُمَّ وَفِّقْهُمْ لِلْخَيْرِ وَالصَّوَابِ، وَاحْفَظْهُمْ مِنَ الْخَطَأِ بِتَقْوَاكَ﴾

23.   Allahumma waffiq-hum lil-khair was-sowsabi, wahfiz-hum minal khatooi bi taqwaaka

O Allah, guide them to good and right, and protect them from error by their piety.

﴿اللّٰهُمَّ اجْعَلْ لَهُمُ الذِّكْرَ الْجَمِيلَ فِي الدُّنْيَا وَالآخِرَةِ، وَأَلْبِسْهُمْ مِنْ مَلَابِسِ الْجَمَالِ وَالْكَمَالِ الْحُلَلَ الْفَاخِرَةَ﴾

24.   Allahummaj`al la-humudh-dhikral jamiila fid-duniyaa wal-aakhirati, wa al-bis-hum min malaabisil jamaali wal kamaalil hulalil faakhirah.

O Allah, grant them the beautiful remembrance in this world and the hereafter, and clothe them in the garments of beauty, and luxury of perfection.

اللَّهُمَّ اجْعَلْهُمْ فِي حِفْظِكَ وَكَنَفِكَ وَأَمَانِكَ وَجَوَارِكَ وَعَيَاذِكَ وَحِزْبِكَ وَحِرْزِكَ وَلُطْفِكَ وَسِتْرِكَ مِنْ كُلِّ شَيْطَانٍ، إِنْسٍ وَجَانٍ، وَبَاغٍ وَحَاسِدٍ، وَمِنْ شَرِّ كُلِّ شَيْءٍ أَنْتَ آخِذٌ بِنَاصِيَتِهِ

25.   Allahumma j'al-hum fii hifzika wakanafika wa amaanika wa jawaarika wa `ayaadhika wa hizbika wa hirzika wa lutfika wa sitrika min kulli shaitooninin insin wa jaanin, wa baaghin wa haasidin, wa min sharri kulli shai'in anta aakhidhun bi naasiatihi.

O Allāh! Place them under Your protection, Your care, Your safety, Your proximity, Your refuge, Your party, your fortification, Your kindness, Your veil from every devil among man and jin, transgressor and envier, and from the evil of everything you hold by its forelock.

اللَّهُمَّ أَكْثِرْ مَالَهُ وَوَلَدَهُ وَبَارِكْ لَهُ فِيمَا أَعْطَيْتَهُ

26.   Allahumma akthir maalahu wa waladahu wa baarik lahu fiimaa a`ataitahu.

O Allah, make an increase in his wealth, and progeny, and confer blessings upon him in everything Thou hast bestowed upon him.

6. Prayer for protection from sins and all evils

اللَّهُمَّ اغْفِرْ ذُنُوبَهُمْ، وَطَهِّرْ قُلُوبَهُمْ، وَحَصِّنْ فُرُوجَهُمْ، وَحَسِّنْ أَخْلاَقَهُمْ، وَامْلأْ قُلُوبَهُمْ نُورًا وَحِكْمَةً، وَأَهِّلْهُمْ لِقَبُولِ كُلِّ نِعْمَةٍ وَاجْعَلْهُمْ مِنَ الذَّاكِرِينَ الْمَذْكُورِينَ، والْطُفْ بِهِمْ يَا كَرِيمُ، وَعَلِّقْ قُلُوبَهُمْ بِطَاعَتِكَ، وَاجْعَلْهُمْ مِنْ أَوْجَهِ مَنْ تَوَجَّهَ إِلَيْكَ وَأَحَبَّكَ

27.   Allahuma gfir dhunuuba-hum wa tohhir quluuba-hum wa hassin furuuja-hum. Wa hassin 'akhlaaqo-hum, wamla' quluuba-hum nuuran wa hikmatan, wa ahhil-hum liqobuli kulli ni'matin waj'al-hum minadh-dhaakiriinal madhkuuriina, waltuf bihim Yaa Kariimu, wa `alliq quluubahum bi too`atika, waj'al-hum min 'aojahi man tawajjaha ilaika wa ahabbaka.

O Allah ! forgive them their sins, purify their souls and preserve their chastity, and grant them good morals. Fill their hearts with light and wisdom, and make them ready to receive every blessing and make them among those who remembers you much and who are also remembered, and grant them your love O the Benevolent. Join their hearts to obedience to You and make them among those who direct their attention to you and Your beloved.

﴿اللَّهُمَّ جَنِّبْهُمْ رُفَقَاءَ السُّوءِ، وَالزِّنَا وَاللِّوَاطَ، وَالْخَمْرَ وَالْمُخَدِّرَاتِ، وَمِنَ الْعِلَلِ وَالْأَوْبِئَةَ وَجَمِيع الْآفَاتِ﴾

28.   Allahumma jannib-hum rufaqaa'as-suu'i, waz-zinaa wal-liwaato, wal-khamro wal-mukhaddirati, wa minal `ilali wal'aobiata wa jamii'il aafaat.

O Allāh! Keep them away from evil companions, fornication, sodomy, alcohol and drugs, and from shortcomings, pandemic and all sins.

﴿اللَّهُمَّ سَلِّمْهُمْ مِنْ شَرِّ الأَشْرَارِ آنَاءَ اللَّيْلِ وَأَطْرَافَ النَّهَارِ، فِي الْإِعْلَانِ وَالْإِسْرَارِ، وَاهْدِهِمْ لِمَا تُحِبُّهُ مِنْهُمْ وَاغْفِرْ لَهُمْ يَا غَفَّارُ.﴾

29.   Allahumma sallim-hum min sharri ashroori aana'al-laili wa atrofan-nahaari, fil 'ilaani wal isroori, wahdi-him limaa tuhibbuhu min-hum waghfir lahum Yaa Ghaffaar.

O Allāh! Deliver them from the evil of the wicked during the night and the ends of the day, in open and secret, and guide them to what You love among them and forgive them.

﴿اللَّهُمَّ جَنِّبْهُمُ الْفَوَاحِشَ وَالْمِحَنَ، مَا ظَهَرَ مِنْهَا وَمَا بَطَنَ﴾

30. Allahumma jannib-humul fawaahisha wal mihana, maa zahara min-haa wa maa batona.

O Allāh! Keep them away from immoralities and trials, the apparent and the hidden among them.

﴿اللَّهُمَّ رَبَّ الْأَرْبَابِ، رَبَّ لِي صَغِيرَهُمْ، وَقَوِّ لِي ضَعِيفَهُمْ، وَعَافِهِمْ فِي أَبْدَانِهِمْ، وَأَسْمَاعِهِمْ، وَأَبْصَارِهِمْ، وَأَنْفُسِهِمْ﴾

31. Allahumma Rabbal arbaabi, Rabba lii soghiiro-hum, wa qawwi lii do`iifa-hum, wa `aafihim fii 'abdaani-him, wa asmaa'i-him, wa absoori-him, wa anfusihim.

O Allāh! Lord of lords, Take care of the small ones among them, and strengthen the weak ones, and grant them health in their bodies, hearings, sights and their souls.

﴿اللَّهُمَّ إِنَّكَ وَهَبْتَ لِي (........) مِنْ غَيْرِ حَوْلٍ مِنِّي وَلاَ قُوَّةَ، فَيَا مَالِكَ الْمُلْكِ وَيَا وَاسِعَ الْعَطَاءِ يَا حَيُّ يَا قَيُّومُ يَا ذَا الْجَلاَلِ وَالإِكْرَامِ أحْفَظْهُمْ بِحِفْظِكَ بِلاَ حَوْلٍ مِنِّي وَلاَ قُوَّةً وَأَسْأَلُكَ فِي هَذَا الْيَوْمِ الْعَظِيمِ وَبِعَدَدِ مَنْ سَجَدَ لَكَ فِي حَرَمِكَ الْمُكَرَّمِ مِنْ يَوْمِ خَلَقْتَ الدُّنْيَا إِلَى يَوْمِ الْقِيَامَةِ أَنْ تَحْفَظَهُمْ مِنْ أَيِّ مَكْرُوهٍ يُصِيبُهُمْ وَمِنْ كُلِّ شَرٍّ وَضَرَرٍ، اللَّهُمَّ وَاحْفَظْهُمْ مِنَ الْأَسْقَامِ وَالْأَمْرَاضِ، اللَّهُمَّ لاَ تَجْعَلْ ابْتِلاَئِي فِيهِمْ، اللَّهُمَّ أَجِرْهُمْ مِنَ الْفِتَنِ مَا ظَهَرَ مِنْهَا وَمَا بَطَنَ﴾

32.   Allahumma innaka wahabta lii (...mention their names...) min gairi haolin min-nii walaa quwwatan, fa Yaa Maalikal Mulki wa Yaa Waasi'al 'ataai, Yaa Hayyun Yaa Qayuum Yaa Dhal Jalaal wal ikraam; Ihfadh - hum bi hifdhika bilaa haolin min nii wa laa quwwah. Wa as'aluka fi haadhal yaomil 'adhiim wa bi 'adadi man sajada laka fii Haramikal Mukarram min yaomin khalaqta-d-dunyaa ilaa yaomil qiyaamah an tahfadha-hum min ayyi makruhin yusiibuhum, wa min kulli sharrin wa dararin. Allahumma ihfadh-hum minal asqaami wal amraad, Allahumma laa taj'al ibtilaa'ii fiihim, Allahumma ajirhum minal fitani maa dhohara minha wa maa batona.

O Allah ! You have blessed me with (...their names) neither by my power nor by my strength. The Sovereign Lord of All-Encompassing bounty, the Ever living and Self Subsistent, the All Besought and Glorified; keep them under Your protection with no other power or strength from me. I ask You on this great day and by the number of prostrations to You in Your sanctuary from the day You created the entire world until the day of resurrection; to save them from any abomination that may afflicts them and from all evils and harms . O Allah! protect them from all diseases and ailments. O Allah! Do not make them my source of trial. O Allah! Safeguard them from all trials either open or secret.

اللَّهُمَّ احْرُسْهُمْ بِعَيْنِكَ الَّتِي لاَ تَنَامُ، وَاكْنُفْهُمْ بِكَنَفِكَ الَّذِي لاَ يُرَامُ، وَاحْفِظْهُمْ بِعِزِّكَ الَّذِي لاَ يُضَامُ، وَاكْلأَهُمْ بِاللَّيْلِ وَالنَّهَارِ، وَأَيِّدْهُمْ بِجَيْشِ الْمَحَبَّةِ، وَاسْقِهِمْ مِنْ شَرَابِ مَحَبَّتِكَ أَكْرَمَ شُرْبَةٍ

33.   Allahumma ahrus-hum bi `ainika llatii laa tanaamu, waknuf-hum bikanafika lladhii laa yuroomu, wahfiz-hum bi `izzika lladhii laa yudoomu, wakla'-hum bil-laili wan-nahaari, wa ayyid-hum bi jaishil mahabbati, wasqihim min sharoobi mahabatika akrama shurbah.

O Allāh, guard them under Your eyes that do not sleep, and protect them with Your protection that is does not fade, and protect them by Your honor that is not disgraced, and guard them by night and by day, and support them with an army of love, and give them to drink from the most honourable drink.

﴿اللَّهُمَّ أَعِذْنَا، وَأَوْلَادِنَا، وَذُرِيَاتِنَا مِنْ فِتْنَةِ الْقَبْرِ وَعَذَابِ النَّارِ، وَمِنْ فِتْنَةِ الْمَحْيَا وَالْمَمَاتِ، وَمِنْ شَرِّ فِتْنَةِ الْمَسِيحِ الدَّجَّالِ ﴾

34.   Allahumma a'idhnaa wa aolaadinaa wa dhuriyaatinaa min 'adhaabil qobri, wa 'adhaabin-naari, wa min fitnatil mahya wal mamaati, wa min sharri fitnatil masiihid-dajjaali.

O Allāh, protect us and our children and progeny from the punishment of the grave, from the torment of the Fire, from the trials and tribulations of life and death and from the evil affliction of Al-Maseeh Ad-Dajjal.

7. Prayer for righteous companions

﴿اللَّهُمَّ ارْزُقْهُمُ الْمُعَلِّمَ الصَّالِحَ، وَالصُّحْبَةَ الطَّيِّبَةَ، وَالْقَنَاعَةَ وَالرِّضَا، وَنَزِّهْ قُلُوبَهُمْ عَنِ التَّعَلُّقِ بِمَنْ دُونَكَ، وَاجْعَلْهُمْ مِمَّنْ تُحِبُّهُمْ وَيُحِبُّونَكَ، وَوَفِّقْهُمْ لِكُلِّ عَمَلٍ يُقَرِّبُهُمْ إِلَى حُبِّكَ ﴾

35.   Allahumma rzuqu-humul mu'allimas-soolih was-suhbatat-tayyibah, wal-qanaa'ata wa r-rido, wa nazzih quluubahum `anit-ta`allaqi biman duunaka, waj'al-hum mimman tuhibbu-hum wa yuhibbuunaka, wawafiq-hum likulli `amalin yuqarribu-hum ilaa hubbika.

O Allah! Grant them pious teachers and righteous associates, and contentment and pleasure. Purify their hearts from relying on other than you. Make them among those whom You love and love You, and grant them every deed that will bring them closer to Your love.

﴿اللَّهُمَّ اكْفِهِمْ بِحَلاَلِكَ عَنْ حَرَامِكَ وَأَغْنِهِمْ بِفَضْلِكَ عَمَّنْ سِوَاكَ﴾

36.   Allahumma kfihim bi halaalika an haroomika waghni-him bi fadlika amman siwaaka.

O Allāh! Suffice them with Your lawful things against Your forbidden things, and enrich them by Your grace with someone other than You.

8. Prayer for steadfastness on the path of truth

﴿اللَّهُمَّ لاَ تُزِغْ قُلُوبَنَا بَعْدَ إِذْ هَدَيْتَنَا وَهَبْ لَنَا مِن لَّدُنْكَ رَحْمَةً، وَهَيِّءْ لَهُمْ مِنْ أَمْرِهِمْ رَشَدًا﴾

37.   Rabbanaa laa tuzigh quluubanaa ba`ada 'idh hadaitanaa wa hab lanaa min ladunka rahmatan wa ahyyi' lahum min amrihim rashadan.

Our Lord, let not our hearts deviate after You have guided us and grant us from Yourself mercy. and facilitate for them their affair in the right way.

﴿اللَّهُمَّ مُنَّ عَلَيَّ بِبَقَاءِ أَوْلاَدِي، وَبِإِصْلاَحِهِمْ لِي، وَبِإِمْتَاعِي بِهِمْ، وَامْدُدْ فِي أَعْمَارِهِمْ، مَعَ الصِّحَّةِ وَالْعَافِيَةِ فِي طَاعَتِكَ وَرِضَاكَ﴾

38. Allahumma munna `alayya bi baqaa'i aolaadii, wabi islaaihi-him lii, wabi imtaa`ii bihim, wamdud fii a`amaari-him, ma`as-sihhati wal `aafiyati fii too`atika wa ridooka.

O Allāh! Bless me with the survival of my children, with their improvement for me, with their enjoyment by me, and grant them longevity, along with health and good condition in obedience to You and Your pleasure.

اللَّهُمَّ اجْعَلْهُمْ لِي مُحِبِّينَ، وَعَلَيَّ مُقْبِلِينَ مُسْتَقِيمِينَ مُطِيعِينَ، غَيْرَ عَاصِينَ وَلاَ عَاقِينَ وَلاَ خَاطِئِينَ.

39.   *Allahumma j'al-hum lii muhibbiina, wa `alayya muqbiliina mustaqimiina muti`iina, ghairo `aasiina wa laa `aaqiina wa laa khooti'iina.*

O Allāh! Make them to love me, and to come to me upright and obedient, and make them not disobedient, disrespectful and undutiful.

اللَّهُمَّ امْنُنْ عَلَيْهِمْ بِكُلِّ مَا يُصْلِحُهُمْ فِي الدُّنْيَا وَالآخِرَةُ، مَا ذَكَرْتُ مِنْهَا وَمَا نَسِيتُ، أَوْ أَظْهَرْتُ أَوْ أَخْفَيْتُ، أَوْ أَعْلَنْتُ أَوْ أَسْرَرْتُ

40.   *Allahumma mnun `alaihim bikulli maa yuslihuhum fid-duniyaa wal aakhirah, maa dhakartu min-haa wa maa nasiitu, ao azhartu ao akhfaitu, ao a'alantu ao asrortu.*

O Allah! Grant them favour in every thing that will improve them in this world and the hereafter, what I mentioned and what I forgot, what I exhibited and what I hid, or declared or kept secret.

9. Prayer for children and parents

رَبِّ أَوْزِعْنِي أَنْ أَشْكُرَ نِعْمَتَكَ الَّتِي أَنْعَمْتَ عَلَيَّ وَعَلَى وَالِدَيَ، وَأَنْ أَعْمَلَ صَالِحًا تَرْضَاهُ، وَأَصْلِحْ لِي فِي ذُرِّيَّتِي، إِنِّي تُبْتُ إِلَيْكَ وَإِنِّي مِنَ الْمُسْلِمِينَ، وَأَعِذْنِي وَذُرِّيَّتِي مِنَ الشَّيْطَانِ الرَّجِيم

41.   *Rabbii aoz`inii an ashkuro n`imataka llatii an`amta `alayya wa `alaa waalidayya, wa an a`mala saalihaan tardoohu wa aslih lii fii dhurriyyatii, innii tubtu ilaika wa innii minal muslimiina. Wa a`iznii wa dhurriyyatii minash-shaitoonir-rajiim.*

"My Lord, enable me to be grateful for Your favor which You have bestowed upon me and upon my parents and to work righteousness of which You will approve and make righteous for me my offspring. Indeed, I have repented to You, and indeed, I am of the Muslims"[5], protect me and my progeny from the accursed devil.

10. Prayer for good training

﴿اللَّهُمَّ أَعِنِّي عَلَى تَرْبِيَتِهِمْ، وَبَرِّهِمْ، وَتَأْدِيبِهِمْ، وَتَعْلِيمِهِمْ﴾

42.   *Allahumma a'innii `alaa tarbiyatihim, wa barrihim, wa ta'dibi-him, wa ta'limi-him.*

O Allāh! Help me to raise them, to honour them, to discipline them, and to teach them.

﴿اللَّهُمَّ إِنِّي رَضِيتُ عَنْ أَوْلَادِي فَارْضَ عَنْهُمْ﴾

43.   *Allahumma innii rodiitu `an aolaadi, fardo `anhum.*

O Allah, I am pleased with my children, so be pleased with them.

﴿اللَّهُمَّ أَعْطِنِي جَمِيعَ ذَلِكَ بِتَوْفِيقِكَ، وَأَعْطِ جَمِيعَ الْمُسْلِمِينَ مِثْلَ الَّذِي سَأَلْتُكَ لِنَفْسِي وَلِأَوْلَادِي﴾

44.   *Allahumma a'tinii jamii'a dhaalika bi tuofiiyiku, wa `ati jamii'al muslimiina mithli lladhi sa'altuka linafsii wali aolaadii.*

O Allah, give me all of those with good luck from You, and give the same things that I requested for myself and my children to all Muslims.

____

[5] Qur'ān 46: 15.

﴿اللَّهُمَّ صَلِّ عَلَى مُحَمَّدٍ وَعَلَى أَزْوَاجِهِ وَذُرِّيَّتِهِ، كَمَا صَلَّيْتَ عَلَى آلِ إِبْرَهِيمٍ، وَبَارِكْ عَلَى مُحَمَّدٍ وَعَلَى أَزْوَاجِهِ وَذُرِّيَّتِهِ، كَمَا بَارَكْتَ عَلَى آلِ إِبْرَهِيمٍ، إِنَّكَ حَمِيدٌ مَجِيدٌ﴾

45.	Allahumma salli 'ala Muhammadin wa 'ala azwaajihi wa dhurriyatihi, kamaa sallaita 'ala aali Ibrahiima. Wa baarik 'ala Muhammadin wa 'ala azwaajihi wa dhurriyatihi, kamaa baarakta 'ala aali Ibrahiima, innaka Hamiidun Majiid.

﴿سُبْحَانَ رَبِّكَ رَبِّ الْعِزَّةِ عَمَّا يَصِفُونَ، وَسَلَامٌ عَلَى الْمُرْسَلِينَ، وَالْحَمْدُ للهِ رَبِّ الْعَالَمِينَ﴾

46.	Subhaanaka Rabbika Rabbil-'izzati 'amma yasifuun. Wa salaamun 'alal mursaliin. Wal hamdulillahi Rabiil- 'aalamiin.

www.ingramcontent.com/pod-product-compliance
Lightning Source LLC
Chambersburg PA
CBHW070328160726
47999CB00003B/1212